T0147163

"When you know what you do, then use this knowledge to do what you now Know."
- Acting House of Healing

APRIL GETZ

THE **TETRAD**

EYES

M.A.G.I.C. Making Authentic Growth Inspiring Change

BALBOA®
PRESS

A DIVISION OF HAY HOUSE

Balboa Press books may be ordered through booksellers or by contacting:

Balboa Press
A Division of Hay House
1663 Liberty Drive
Bloomington, IN 47403
www.balboapress.com
1 (877) 407-4847

Because of the dynamic nature of the Internet, any web addresses or
links contained in this book may have changed since publication and
may no longer be valid. The views expressed in this work are solely those
of the author and do not necessarily reflect the views of the publisher,
and the publisher hereby disclaims any responsibility for them.

The author of this book does not dispense medical advice or prescribe the use
of any technique as a form of treatment for physical, emotional, or medical
problems without the advice of a physician, either directly or indirectly. The
intent of the author is only to offer information of a general nature to help
you in your quest for emotional and spiritual well-being. In the event you use
any of the information in this book for yourself, which is your constitutional
right, the author and the publisher assume no responsibility for your actions.

Any people depicted in stock imagery provided by Thinkstock are
models, and such images are being used for illustrative purposes only.
Certain stock imagery © Thinkstock.

Print information available on the last page.

ISBN: 978-1-5043-5752-4 (sc)
ISBN: 978-1-5043-5751-7 (e)

Library of Congress Control Number: 2016907369

Balboa Press rev. date: 07/14/2016

DEDICATION

To Larrie Pilling, who changed my life dramatically. Your teachings gave me deep meaning. Your example of dedication and commitment inspired me to commit. I will always be grateful.

To Gary Ogilvie, who allowed me to see the profound impact a poem can have and gave me the ending of the poem that showed the love. This is grace.

To my daughter, Morgyn Laine Getz, who inspires me in so many ways. Your big heart and giving nature never end. I remember the first time I saw your spirit. It was when we went hiking and you were about three years old. In the mountains along the path, you ran ahead and picked up a leaf with a raindrop on it and carefully walked back to give it to me, and you said, "Here, Mom, a little drink for you."

To my son, Konrad Leon Getz, who taught me about truth. Your ability to see the truth gave me strength to get through difficult times.

To Bonnie Carlson, who as a dear friend always supported me, no matter what. The many sharings in the backyard kept me going.

To Corrine Watson, who as a dear friend showed me how being a good mother makes all the difference.

To my brother, Mark Bicknell. You always opened up your life to include me, no matter what was going on, and provided a safe place to land where I could just be.

To Mandy Bicknell, my sister-in-law who always loved me in all that I am.

To Marnie Smith, who as a very dear friend allowed me to experiment with the system to have the big aha moments. Thank you for this bridge to heal others; you are a founding participant whom I will always be grateful for.

To Cally, our kitty cat, for always resting on my belly when I needed warmth and compassion.

To Leah Bicknell, my sister, for showing me the way out of ego.

To Jean Bicknell, my mother, for showing me my beauty.

To my father, Robert Thurston Bicknell, for showing me the softness in a man.

To Louise L. Hay. Your little book *Heal Your Body* was my great inspiration to be a teacher.

FOREWORD

April Getz has provided an extraordinary route for personal reflection. A way to get out of distortion in your mind to a more balanced focus. *The Tetrad Eyes* is like your own personal diamond. I be, I am, I say, and I do connects thoughts that you didn't realize you needed to unite at these points. This is a foundation for internal harmony resonating with your own core values. By using the illustrations with your own thought patterns, you will gain insight for more comfort in your life.

April has led me to understand my own discomfort. I can attest to the benefits of this system as well as the healing from the poetry. I am very appreciative of my own learnings, and I feel this is of great value to others. The relief from old thought patterns has enabled me to be an enhanced contributor in my relationships in all areas of my life.

This is more important now in times of uncertainty. This approach of whole-mind learning has had more of an impact for change in my life. I will recommend *The*

Tetrad Eyes wholeheartedly to anyone as a valued resource for a better-quality life.

Marnie Smith
Calgary, Alberta, Canada

PREFACE

This book is inspired by six years of working with a system I call "The Tetrad Eyes." I was looking for something to feel comfortable connecting my mind and my heart. In my twenty-five years of marriage, the question always came up for me: Why do I not feel good? I just didn't know what to do. I tried journaling and found the same garbage coming out on paper that was rambling around in my mind. This journaling was the beginning of seeing my issues on paper.

My continued search for the knowledge to settle down the restless part of myself led me to Personal Best Seminars in Calgary, Mastery of Self Expression in Vancouver, and finally Peak Potentials with T. Harv Ecker in Calgary. This learning was over a two-year period (1999–2001). I tried bungee jumping, I tried stand-up comedy, and I climbed a mountain to hang off a cliff face. I also walked on fire. These experiences all came from the personal development over the years. All of these things gave me more knowledge about myself, but there was still the pull longing for more. I have always said there has got to be an easier way.

Seriously, People

Over the next year, my marriage became uncomfortable. I was so unhappy, and I could see and feel that my marriage wasn't working. The counseling didn't work either. I could see the spirits in my children being squashed out. This actually was my motivator to get out. I felt so alone and scared, but when I saw the lights going out in my children as well as my spouse, I knew I had to be the strong one, to leave and allow each of us to have a healthier, more fulfilling life.

The next couple of years, I was very busy with the children in sports. The divorce was smooth but not without a lot of pain. The many tears have created the space for growth. Things settled down, and this voice kept coming back: *April, there is more.*

I have also thought, *Do I have to have a crisis to realize what I need to do?* I love helping others in all areas of my life, but where was I really making a difference?

At this point, I was looking inside and thirsted for more self-knowledge. I found Larrie Pilling, who worked with me for six years. Larrie was experimenting and developing a whole-mind learning system. He said that he needed me to be his student to teach. I was so excited. I began working two times a week with the system. I evolved as my own inner teacher, and things really began to change in my life. I got to see myself through this system, which seems to take away the pressure somehow.

This system is designed to show your mind what makes sense and then to bring the feelings along for a connected healing. My first healing was that I didn't need outside validation anymore. The most impactful was that everyone around me was a reflection of what was going on inside me. This experience was really quite remarkable for me. I continued to explore and healed the part of me that was an over-taker and the part of me that was an over-giver. These dysfunctions occurred in different parts of me that I couldn't see before. I also have had many experiences of being alone, wanting someone else to fill that space.

I finally got it: No one can give me wholeness; I can only give that to myself. To be all one. My experiences with men over the last ten years have healed this part of myself that used to rely on the statement that *you* complete me. I used the system to come to this knowing.

I worked directly with Larrie for six years, and for the last three years, I have been working with this system on my own. I have a deep desire to share it with others. If you experience some healings as I have, then this is the purpose of this project.

I have found that using the system is a personal thing, that each individual can choose how to incorporate the knowledge into their lives. My experience is that the work is intimate; it can be learned privately within each person.

I just need to get this out to people and allow them the wonderful healing that is a natural fallout of using these tools. If there is a way to incorporate the learnings from all my most valued teachers, then so be it.

My teachers are many. Here are some of the authors from whom I've learned: John Bradshaw, Caroline Myss, Steven Covey, Sylvia Brown, Pam Grout, Wayne Dyer, Don Miguel Ruiz, Marianne Williamson, Doreen Virtue, Paulo Coelho, Gerry Gavin, Louise L. Hay, Gary Zukav, Deepak Chopra, Carl Weschcke and Joe Slate, Susan Campbell, and Ester and Jerry Hicks.

This is a simple system to guide your awareness to the distorted mind thoughts. The poetry added to this book serves as a guide to the healthier feeling state. The intent is to see the thoughts and the feelings that are driving your life.

What Does It Matter?

This is a story of a time in my life when I really felt like I did not matter.

It was 2004, and I had been on my own for a couple of years. I divorced after twenty-five years of marriage. I really had no idea what was in store for me, but I knew I had to leave the marriage because my spirit was dying and I could see the effects of the dysfunctional marriage on my children. I was always someone who did things for everyone else, and that was how I gauged my existence. My identity was outside of myself.

I wanted to experience giving without expecting in return.

My life was so full of busy-ness, and I never felt that I mattered. I felt like what I did was making a difference, but I needed to matter to someone as me.

I decided to visit the "Drop-In Center" here in Calgary. I made an appointment with Yolanda, a counselor there. I asked Yolanda to give me scenarios of two homeless people, a woman and a man. She described each person, and I was attracted to helping Homeless Man because he was in a two-year recovery program for addicts. The woman was not. At that moment, I asked Yolanda if I could help Homeless Man directly. I would bring cash to her monthly, and she would choose how the money would be used to help him. I remember leaving the center that day very clearly. I had a rush of constant chills going up and down my spine while driving home that day. I knew this was a good thing to do, and I felt really good.

I continued to go once a month for about four months. Yolanda would tell me that she bought him some boots or a bus pass—whatever he needed to keep him on track. She reported that he was doing well after being in the program for about a year. He was working now, and he had a goal to visit his family in Vancouver at the end of the year for Christmas.

Homeless Man lost his family due to a cocaine addiction. He had two children.

I loved to hear about his progress, but something was missing for me. I asked her if it would be okay if Homeless Man and I wrote to each other.

When he wrote, he addressed the letters to "Angel." His letters were a profound experience for me because I felt what it was like to be him through his words. Homeless Man was actually a very good writer; he had lovely handwriting and was articulate. I never offered advice, only the space for him to express his feelings.

Many times, I would read the letters over and over again. I would cry so much and wonder how someone could experience all this pain and addiction and have no one to talk to. You see, his parents had been addicts, and his wife had been as well. The darkness and hopelessness was at times overwhelming. I really began to see that the things in my life that were causing me grief were small compared to this.

He showed me a lot of gratitude. I want to say I cannot tell you how much that meant to me, but I can: It made a huge difference to me to have this kind of effect on one man's life. We continued to write letters for the next few months.

Yolanda began sharing with me the profound difference she was seeing in Homeless Man. He was making great progress and was soon ready to leave for Vancouver. Time was moving quickly, and it was the end of the year. Homeless Man was finally going to Vancouver to see his children.

He was given permission to visit and spend Christmas dinner with his children.

I met Yolanda and wanted to give more than $100 because I received a bonus at work. I gave $300 to Yolanda; she purchased some bus passes and grocery coupons for Homeless Man for his stay in Vancouver.

The letter I received from Homeless Man after Christmas was one of the most beautiful things in my life. Homeless Man shared that he had spent all the grocery coupons on Christmas dinner, which he surprised his family with. He said it had been a very long time since he had felt so proud to provide. Homeless Man has since recovered and was able to get a job near his family.

Yolanda and I met for one last time. We talked about the journey that we all went through. There was a moment when no words could describe this shared experience. We just looked into each other's eyes and felt something special.

That was when I knew I mattered.

This gave me the connection to a bigger part within and to the outside world.

INTRODUCTION

The "I be I am I say I do" system is a *bridge* to your M.A.G.I.C.

Making **A**uthentic **G**rowth **I**nspire **C**hange from

I've been … I was … I said … I did …

This is what I be, therefore I am, and then I say to you that which brings in what I do.

The definitions of *transformation* and *transform* imply a major change in form, nature, or function. *Convert* implies a change that fits something for a new or different use. The transformation many times was not in my awareness; therefore, the life I was living was uncomfortable.

The Tetrad Eyes will guide you to a higher self-awareness. You will learn about perspectives. The tools are available to use for yourself, to claim your own internal gift to share with the world. Sharing the poems along the way is a different perspective of bringing the heart and mind together.

TESTIMONIALS

April's poems empower and inspire people to act. One poem in particular, "I Should," impacted me so much that I quickly changed my career to one that enables me to live my life based on my purpose!

—Vincenzo Aliberti, Ph.D.
Founder, The Peak Success Institute
Calgary, Alberta, Canada

CONTENTS

HOLD ON OR CONNECT

In the space of the old 4 aspects of self of "I have been and I was and I said and I did," suggests that you are holding on.

To hold on means that I am afraid of losing something, to which I ask, *What is it that I am losing?*

Maybe it is not this at all. Maybe it is just a feeling of stress or pain that has no place to go. The consistent message of letting go is the opposite of holding on. What if you don't have to let go of anything? Maybe this feeling was just part of the original dysfunctional thought to find a way to connect rather than let go.

All the experience of holding on now has a new face to serve as a bridge to something bigger, something more. It seems that holding on is one-sided. It is only you who can hang in there. Who likes to hang in there? Consider a connection, a joining or fastening together rather than either holding on or letting go.

An experience of connection utilizes every part of a whole-brain learner. Connection recognizes the importance of every single detail to allow for the connection. Being connected means that the resources are made available for a richer, fuller experience.

You are not letting go of anything. Everything up to this moment supported the next step, the next movement. The feeling does not suggest loss; it suggests that you have put in place that which is required for your evolution.

Have you ever had an experience of holding on to a relationship or a job and feel that the more you held on, the harder it got to hang in there? In connection, the whole brain involves all parts that communicate with each other in a congruent way. Each part of the aspect of self in "I be I am I say and I do" has an interdependence. For example, in the aspect of self at "I say," you say to yourself, "I will not say that because it will hurt a person's feelings," but when you stay quiet, you are hurting yourself.

LET'S GET CONNECTED

The purpose of this section is to see ways to connect. When I can see that you and I have something in common, this is a draw to get to know each other more, an invitation to connect to you at all aspects of yourself—the beingness, or language, or what you identify with and how you act.

Disconnected is not what any one of us wants to be. Our whole person is sacred due to our unique experiences. My teachers are out there, and many of them tell us to look within for our own healing.

I think this is wonderful and useful, but the thing that keeps coming back to my little head is that if I am wearing the same glasses and looking within, I see the same thing. So how do I change this? How do I change my perspective? Learning is a lifelong journey, and learning about ourselves is especially challenging. There is no university degree to obtain. There is no outline to follow or even a guarantee to fall back on. The results stay the same in my life because I have the same view.

I feel separate, or I try really hard. For me, I try really hard and study to get this or get that, just keep getting stuff. I still feel bad, so I read another trillion books. I wonder if I need to have a tragedy in my life in order to find my "so-called purpose." Or do I need to be a super-high achiever? There are so many people in the middle, in-between the two, and what do I have to offer, I wonder?

So it is you and I, people in the middle who are being overlooked. We are a huge part of helping this planet become whole. I want to be connected. I want to share what I know. I want things to be easier for you.

I have a new perspective on each of the following aspects of myself, which you might relate to:

I could be the same as you in the respect that I had alcoholic parents and they taught me what they could.

I could be the same in the respect that I have felt alone even when I was married for twenty-five years.

I could be the same in the respect that I have had many failed relationships for these last twelve years.

I could be the same in the respect that I lived with the belief that I was stupid.

I could be the same in the respect that I thought my identity was tied to what I was for everyone else.

I could be the same in the respect that I was a taker; I felt things were owed to me.

I could be the same in the respect that my husband and I had a son who was critically ill, and we lost ourselves.

I could be the same in the respect that I let others take advantage of me financially and physically.

I could be the same in the respect that I liked to write simple poems and kept this gift to myself.

I could be the same in that I have lost my job three times in the last three years.

A unified world through one's act of connection. These are wonderful words, but how?

My friends, consider this—You know what you do ... right? Well, through learning and observing, you then *do what you know.* This is where the change occurs.

This is the internal connection. This system, where you recognize the area of disconnection within yourself at the four aspects I be, I am, I say, and I do, will show you where you want to feel better. This is the motivation for change.

What do I know about what I am doing? To do requires courage, but not much. You have to live with yourself, so why not make a change? Is this easy? Yes, of course it is really easy, and a quick fix with a full guarantee that you can go back to the way you were if that is your choice.

Does this system require preparation? It is not an app or a quick email, but if you gain a quick insight to change the smallest thing, then that is a reward to build on.

Everything is multidimensional in life. I am part of life, so if I look at myself with multidimensional tools, perhaps the potential change will resonate with me more at a natural level.

These tools allowed me to reach my inner wisdom from a logical and feeling level. The combination is of heart and mind.

Your journey to happiness and a fulfilling life starts with self-awareness. This book explores four aspects of self: being, language, identity, and actions.

In the tetrad program, these are called, respectively, *I be, I say, I am,* and *I do.*

The program is a multidimensional path to self-healing. It will take you on a journey of personal discovery at each aspect of self, the premise being that until we are whole and healthy in all four aspects, we will always feel as if something is missing and not be able to lead the fulfilling life we deserve.

The key to this system is to allow for new growth. It could be uncomfortable, like sitting in a chair with one leg shorter than the other three.

My mind is receptive to this system because it makes sense. Then I allow myself to feel at each point of change, providing the bridge to change. New actions, new behaviors.

There are three levels to the system:

1. See where you are in a negative state.
2. See what you desire in the positive.
3. Come to a conclusion of a good outcome.

The thoughts that the mind generates at the point of a good outcome will give you a good feeling that allows for new actions.

What does it mean to say, "You know what you do, and then do what you know"?

What this means is when you look at the first level (Negative Thinking) of "I be, I am, I say, and I do," you will see the area that you are distorted in. This is the point of understanding what you are doing in your life to cause bad feelings. (This is where you feel those aspects of self—you know what you do.)

The illustration shows an example of negative thinking at the aspect of self in "I say." It is Fear Level 1—you are in fear.

Then go to the second level (Path to Healing) of "I be, I am, I say, and I do" and you will see a healing. Let's look at the aspect of "I say." Level 1—you are in fear. Level 2—you are in confrontation.

Then go to the third level (Healing Transformation). This is the reconciliation.

1. You are in fear.
2. You are in confrontation.
3. You are in truth.

Know what you do (fear)—move across the bridge (confrontation)—do what you know (speak the truth)

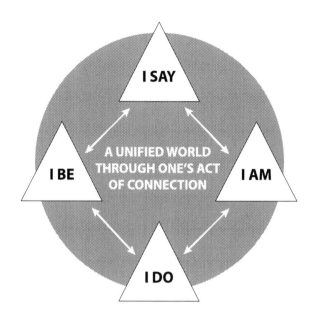

I BE

I AM

I SAY

I DO

"A unified world through one's act of connection"

"You know what you do. Then you *do* what you *know*."

The human mind is so rigid that it cannot accept anything that does not conform to it. The Tetrad Eyes shows the way for the mind to conform by looking at the four aspects of self.

WHY SYMBOLS

The following is an explanation of the symbols used to represent the four aspects of self:

1. In a circle, Monad represents the whole that holds all four aspects of self—oneness - See Full Integrity Circle

2. The Dyad is a description of a relationship between two points, for example, Toxic Shame and Healthy Shame. – See Full Integrity Circle

3. The Triad is a reconciliation of the two points, for example, Toxic Shame to Healthy Shame reconciled at Salvation - See Full Integrity Circle

4. The Tetrad is a group of four produced by the successive divisions of a cell. All 4 points of self-reconciled. See Full Integrity Circle.

1. **Monad—EGO It's all about me separately. Unless I have self-unity, what difference does it make what I decide to do?**

- Monad universality—meaning all-encompassing

- Totality—meaning the total of all of the parts within

- Unity in diversity- meaning the whole becomes stronger in the differences

- In grasping Monad, an act is required that goes beyond knowing.

- This act makes a connection between two real structures.

- Interrelated interdependence

2. **Dyad**—Unity can arise only from conscious duality. Opposites complement each other.

Dyad, if stuck in polarity, keeps separateness, right/ wrong, either/or. I give up ownership, I am not responsible for myself.

The human mind is so rigid that it cannot accept anything that it does not conform to, that it hasn't previously experienced or learned, or that it does not consider reasonable—*a major block to reaching a higher level of consciousness.*

- A divided mind is weak. A united mind is clear, singular in purpose, and powerful beyond measure.

- Unity is determined by the sovereignty of each element.

- We appreciate diverse attributes of each other; therefore, we teach at a higher level, encompassing the value of each contrast. This applies within and outside ourselves.

- Awareness of differences by contrast

- The tension between two opposing domains is potentially dynamic.

- The greater the discernment of duality, the more strength to bear the opposites.

- Starkness of irreconcilable differences must be accepted.

- Right and left hemispheres

3. **Triad**—Law of three—Law of dynamism—Conditions that make resolution possible—Impulse that draws together the Reconciling force. Corpus callosum

is the band of commissural fibers uniting the cerebral hemispheres.

The negative triad creates a power-hungry, self-centered individual who ignores the possibility of reconciliation.

- Amazing skill which utilizes the gift of how we can keep up with information overload and rapidly changing times.

- Right hemisphere capacity for being acted upon undergoing an effect.

- Left hemisphere impulse that acts upon—ability to act, produce an effect.

4. Tetrad—Form of all activities that perpetuate order

Victim—the power victimizer is irresponsible and immature and feels more than human. The passive victimizer feels less than human.

The Tetrad forms the constituents of our fundamental course. Based on J.G. Bennett's work on systematics, a tool for understanding wholes.

FEELINGS ARE DRIVERS

Your emotions are a reaction to your mind's thoughts, and your feelings are the truth. From *The Essential Law of Attraction Collection*, by Esther and Jerry Hicks

The Tetrad Eyes has four perspectives. (See the feelings that are attached to the words.)

I know that thoughts are the basis of the feelings.

The example noted below uses only the "Female Energy" in the illustrations. You can do the "Male Energy" by following this example in the Full Circle.

Start: Negative thought is "I am stupid" or "I need approval." See Negative Illustration.

For example, if the Female Energy of "I be" feels Toxic Shame, then part of me (I am) feels Toxic Guilt, "I say" feels apathy, and then "I do" (I do nothing)—I grieve for myself.

The Tetrad of negative thinking is an illustration to see the words at each point of self. The words at each point of self in negative thinking affect each other. For example, at "I be," when I feel ashamed, then at "I am" I feel guilty, and at "I say" I feel suppressed or apathetic, and at "I do" I feel grief. These points are all tied together. This is looking at the whole self at once.

For example: If I hold a belief of being stupid, then I feel guilty about not being able to accomplish the task at hand. Then I will not say anything and will sit in grief and do nothing.

The result is stifling.

Movement: Here is an example of a Path to Healing thought "I can learn." See Path to Healing Illustration.

The Tetrad of Path to Healing is an illustration to see the words at each point of self. The words at each point of self in Path to Healing affect each other. For example, at "I be," when I feel Healthy Shame, this thought simply means other options become available to me when I tell myself *I can learn*. Then at "I am," I have a responsibility to myself to take the time to learn. And at "I say," I have the feeling of self-endorsement because I am smart enough to look for answers. At "I do" I celebrate the action of doing.

The result is movement freeing.

Reconciled Self: Full Circle—"I can learn" thought is now complete.

The Tetrad of Full Circle is an illustration to see the words at each point of self. The words at each point of self in Full Circle affect each other. For example, at "I be," when I feel Salvation, I learned. Then at "I am," I am redeemed at my identity. And at "I say" I have a feeling of forgiveness to let go of being hard on myself. At "I do" I surrender to the outcome, knowing I have done my best.

The result is balance.

Full Integrity the Cover Circle. The four aspects of self have moved from "Negative Thinking" to "Path to Healing" to a point of reconciliation at "Full Integrity" of the whole self.

I be—Salvation and liberation from clinging to the world of appearance and final union with ultimate reality, the saving of man from the power and effect of sin, and preservation from the destruction of failure. Mercy is a blessing that is an act of divine favor or compassion—a compassion shown to victims of misfortune.

I am—Redemption is to release from blame or doubt and to free from the bondage of sin. When you reclaim your thoughts and do not live up to obligation, you can convert to being humble rather than arrogant.

I say—Forgiveness is to cease feeling resentment and gain a feeling of relief. The truth becomes clear.

I do—Surrender, to give up completely to one's self-guidance, is to yield to the power of inner truth. Gratitude—Freedom from care or desire—contentment of benefits received.

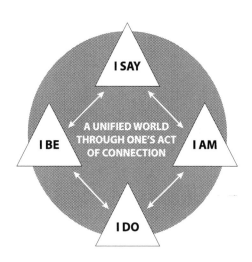

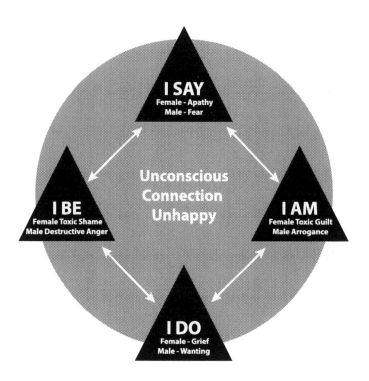

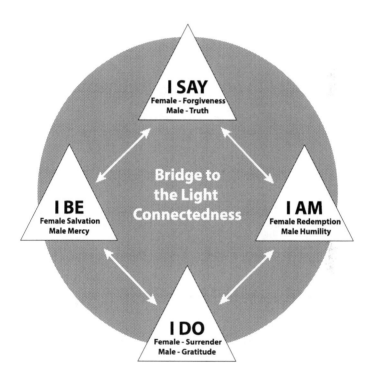

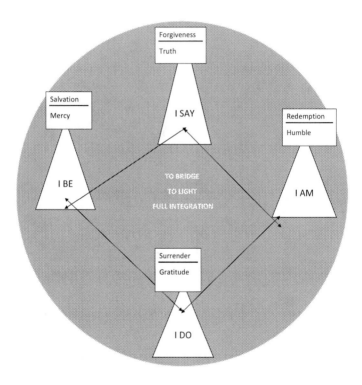

QUESTIONS FOR YOU

The questions below are to open the mind.

1. What do you think it would take for someone to
    receive the benefits of using this system?

    Allowing yourself to experience the system will
    show you the benefits. Simply take one area that
    you would like to work with and do it. Take, for
    example, the old thought pattern of "I am stupid."
    I replaced it with "There is always a way." By
    replacing this thought, the outcome is a resolution
    and an increased self-confidence. Transformation
    happens in little things, a little at a time.

2. Is this easy to do? I have so much to do as it is.

    The system is only a point of reference for you to
    use by watching your thoughts daily, especially
    when you feel bad. The diagrams of moving from
    Negative Thinking to Path to Healing to Full
    Circle will open the mind to good thoughts.

3. What do people have to do to get ready to use this system?

   There is no getting ready. You are here looking at the system because you are ready.

4. Where did the answers come from for your healing?

   The system allowed me to access my own inner wisdom. I know this sounds clichéd, but simple makes sense. Going back home or becoming authentic is freeing, simple.

5. Is this too complicated for people to use?

   I guess it would be like not having a connection. Once you see and experience how the pieces of the four aspects of yourself fit together, then your changes become easy.

6. So people use this system and are fixed, and then leave it alone. Sort of like having surgery—problem removed and life is great. What are your thoughts on this?

   I think allowing for new growth is the approach of this system. Eventually the weeds cannot grow.

7. What impact did some of these healings have on your life, relationships, work, health, etc.?

The same old thoughts played over and over again. I just replaced them within the system.

Who doesn't like salvation, redemption, forgiveness, and gratitude? I admit, moving to these points caused some tears, but the realization enabled me to create a new belief.

8. Why do you think the poems are shared with this system?

The four dimensions of self are complemented by the balance of mind and heart. To help you, the reader, connect the logical aspects of the program with the emotional breakthroughs you will make, I have included poems that I wrote that helped me along my own journey.

9. How much time does it take to benefit from this system?

This is a personal experience for everyone. For myself, to let go of the label "stupid," I had to experience a hacker breaking into my computer; then a security system that didn't work; then I called for help, only to find it wouldn't be available until two weeks down the road. I decided to connect to the system, let go of the old mantra in my head, and replace it with "I can figure this out" and "I am not alone." As I did this, I noticed that I became calmer. I then reinstalled Windows on my computer and reinstalled Outlook and the original security system, the whole time trusting that it would work out. And it did. My observer decided to do what I know now.

10. Why do you think people can use this system?

There really is no limit to what a person could do to redesign it for their own personal healing; working with these tools is a choice.

11. What gives the system substance and longevity?

Different situations come into life. The circumstances that are uncomfortable bring me to the four aspects of myself over and over again. One example is when I was let go from a job. It was abrupt, and it hurt a lot. I went back to the four aspects of myself and learned that when I felt wronged, I could have spoken up. I wasn't being true to myself. This awareness was worth it for my self-preservation.

12. How would you encourage people to make using the system a priority?

It is very empowering to have something that you can count on. The system has worked for me many times, and I only want to share. I feel very passionate about being my own teacher, and I want to offer you a new perspective. This is a different way for you to embrace your own teacher.

It is my greatest desire for you to experience more goodness in your life.

13. Did you have to experience a life-altering challenge to look at different ways to heal yourself? Or do you think everyone can use this?

   As I have said before, I think the little transformations are the key. For me, a catastrophic event did not have to happen, for which I am eternally grateful.

14. What if you don't follow everything to a T in the system? Do you think you still gain?

   Yes. It's like trying on a new outfit: At first, you may feel uncomfortable, but that is normal. Work with what feels right and trust that there is no "right" way, only your way. Sometimes receiving calmness or seeing your own beauty is unsettling.

POEMS

Heart of Many Layers

I am blessed to have you in my life.
It is a rare experience to have a friendship of this height
We have laughed together many a time—In New York,
a trophy moment.
On the bus home from a golf tournament was also potent.
I feel so good around you; I know that I can count on you.
If I were to go through life with one friend, I am proud
because it is you.
We have cried together and shared deep and painful times,
Healing in exchange of our words, and maybe a little wine.
We have taken many walks on the reservoir or in the woods,
Always a special exchange, confirming what we can and could,
Not blocking growth or staying stuck, we lift each other up.
Your intelligence and beauty—sometimes I am awestruck.
Using your heart and your eyes to see keeps me moving
when I couldn't be free.
So it is sixty years you have been on this earth,
I think your soul is timeless, and the years are jewels in
your purse.
For you are a treasure, a pleasure, no measure to meet

A light, a voice, a hug. Unique.
The words are only a small part to say
Thank you, my friend, forever and a day.

Your friend,
April

Emma—Angel in Human Form

You are flying from the nest on to more and better, to
be your best;
Remember who you are in the open world when taken
to the test.
Emma, you are a dedicated loving person who cares for
all in your path.
Direct this inside and you will be protected from wrath.
I have seen it so many times, and you show it with a smile:
You give from the heart with your own style.

Your inner guide is your light and source;
Hold onto this when things go off course.

Great opportunity lies ahead,
Offering excitement uncertainty and you will be led,
Your chance to show another divine part of you,
Unveiling the flower, your beauty, in what you do.
I know you will be successful because you already are,
Even when your friends are not close and so far.

Our hearts are with you on this new dream in life.
It will be easy and flowing because the time is right.
Love, April
Thank you for everything

Mom, Me

Souls are born new and renewed
As reflection in the mirror or in you.
A seedling grows, and you see yourself,
Only better this time, of which I have not felt.
Life gives, and some same things dealt.
So a message comes, from where we can only guess;
Perhaps it is the place where we go to rest.
The words aren't there, but the feelings are strong—
That we are all created equal, there is no wrong.
The love goes deeper than we can ever know
Until we look closely and it begins to show.
My heart aches for the love that has been lost,
But it is never too late, because this bridge I can cross.
I see you and you see me through our eyes;
To look for the greatness is what seals the ties.
Oh, I love you, Mom, forever and a day.
I know how you feel and what you want to say,
So just hold me close and rejoice in our good.
Let Mother Nature and Father Time allow things to be
as they should.

Fit In

The Girl Who Wants to Fit In
I am doing what I think is right to fit in.
I see you people and look for the space of win,
I look at other people to see where I fit in.
Show you that I am like you, and you will connect with me.
Please see that we are one and more power as we.
However, I am confused about what is next;
How do I get in and be a part of what is best?

Trying harder and going faster, I am driven,
Ignoring myself and that which is given.
What is it I am not seeing in this storm of emotion?
My head keeps telling me the ways of motion,
Stirring and twirling of the thought of notion.
I feel the trauma of being not real,
Looking for moments of truth to steal.

My body gives out, and there is no more.
The true dealer of truth brings me to the floor.
Past behavior doesn't work anymore.

What has worked before is gone, but why?
I don't know what to do, so I sit and cry.

The wall I hit and no place to go.
I let go of compassion and was gripped by control.

My heart is pounding to be heard right now.
Is it stronger than my mind, that one I allow?

I scramble and look to others for my answer,
Find out they too have the same disaster.
This is not the way of the heart.
Must release and find my start.

Detach, I say, and go within—seek inner knowledge to
release the sin,
Look to love of self and gift to others for the reflection
within.

How do I fit in? I say.
I want to be truthful in all that I say.
The gift I receive, I need to give it away.

Help with I Do

Marry yourself on this path to a healthier lifestyle,
Don't worry about the past or where
you've been this last while.
Just remember, the trainer holds everything in view,
Paving the way for balance and renew.
One who really sees the person—is the
one who can be that person,
Relating to experiences creates connection;
Let's build together the vision or intention.
Sometimes we need help to make a change,
Setting up the place and the needed stage.
Eyes can guide from the outside
To get stronger with one by your side.
Combining the whole picture is the magic of a master,
To help each individual work harder and get there faster.
A warm heart is another great addition—
Helps heal each step for a bigger rendition.
Trusting the trainer, for your wellness is kept whole,
A commitment of passion and to those it will show.
It will fall into areas of your life as a surprise,
Letting go of many places of relenting demise.
Walk tall, my friend, and feel the difference—
Self-confidence, respect, and finally acceptance.

I Am

I am innocent and pure, full of joy I see on other faces.
I am a tiny body of power, and I play just living and being.
No matter where I go, there are smiles from all places.
My eyes are open, yet it's only with my heart that I am seeing.
I feel free and loved … In being, I give without having to try.
I enjoy the moments flowing, it's okay to laugh and it's
okay to cry.

I stumble around getting to know my space.
I fall and get up, trusting in my place.

I giggle and fall and say, "Hi, my name is April."
At two years old, I am tall inside, say, "Look at me! I am
pretty special!"
As I get bigger on the outside, I get smaller on the inside.
The others say, "Stop that. Be quiet. Be careful. Get out
of my way."
I learned not to be me anymore—it was not okay.
I learned to get love—there was always a price.
I learned to be funny—I thought this was right.

As a teen, I rebelled a lot, said, "Look at me!
Isn't it okay? Just look, you will see.
I know I am good, but why won't you love me?
What is it about me that they cannot see?"
I continue with this mask; it has worked so good.
What the hell do I do? I do what I should.

My soul continued to cry, cry even louder.
I can't take this anymore. I am me and I have to be.

I know I am not happy and not willing to settle.
I can't be like them, drowning in the bottle.
I look at my daughter and son who need me now;
I will not abandon them, will be strong, but how?
I've looked for love outside for so long,
It keeps coming back to within, lives my song.

So here I sit in this internal storm. I can't continue to blame anymore.
How do I do it? Where is this magic door?
God shrink me down to when I was two,
A time when I knew who was who,
I walk tall, proud of me, saying, "Hi, I am April. Look at me."
I will accept you no matter what you say, because we are all
Alike. God made us this way.

The lines in my face show pain and laughs.
I have given so much on this worthy path.
I cannot change who I am, you see,
It is time to let go and let me be me.
I will rest and love, only be for now,
Because that is the gift to share, that is how.

I Be I Am I Say I Do

To understand the journey inwards
Is like expressing and being grateful without words.
You can see with your eyes only so much,
Then you bring in the heart what the eyes cannot touch.
Is there a greater gift than to know oneself,
To be your own guide and create inner wealth,
Trusting with no question and watch faith take the lead?
What is this connection, this constant
urge to always nurture the seed?
The will for one to be with all
Is innate, to be heard and be welcomed by all.

It's Not Just a Process

I remember the day that Al introduced you.
You seemed so quiet and subdued.
Did my judgment come out to put you in a box?
Yes, she did, and what a paradox.
You worked very hard and built a place for JV to stand,
Learning about oil and gas and the stuff about the land,
Keeping all the kitties in the corral
when things went astray,
Leading with knowledge, compassion,
and making your way.
You said, "April, stop helping
everyone look closer today."
I had a hard time letting go of this, being the one to say
I liked people coming to me for guidance and play.
The benefits showed up right away.
You recognized that I need to create and speak,
Designing the JE and reconciliations to steep.
Quick-fix, big-picture, a habit of mine
Put me in an emotional bind.
You took the lead and guided me through;
That was when my loyalty came true.
A tear and some red in my face;
Thank you for noticing I am human with grace.
I want to sing that song—to her with love—
But that would sound funny, I know,
Reaping the lesson you did sow.
Forever I will cherish and will always grow
A little sprinkle of the effect you had on me;

Just wanted to share so everyone could see.
You will be missed, Joan, but we wish you the best.
Keep your pep and smile and your lightning zest.

Hugs April Getz

Olivia

Everyone needs to know that they are grand,
Even when faced with weakness, and it is hard to stand.
When faced with a choice and you
are shaking and scared,
Look at the bear and know that you are heard.
Put him in a special place to remind you every day:
You bring light and joy to others in what you say.

The universe gives you your very own
planet, your very own world,
So take off, Olivia, and make this your
place, your own treasure to hold.
Sometimes it gets dark and you cannot see your way,
Trust the Fairy who loves you and guides you this day.
Remember to follow your heart—the truth from inside
Light the candle and listen to your own trusted guide

Laugh out loud and be who you are;
This will heal the heart and mend the scar.
Your light, your love shines in all that you do.
The pure kind person shines through and through.

Merry Christmas, Olivia
Angel

Reid and Abbie

For many years you have been important in my life, Reid.
You are a part of Morgyn and a part of Konrad, the love
that you feed.
You always had and still do have the loving, kind ways.
This is a foundation for the years full of long and happy days.

Memories of young Reid play an important part
For the new path, the new start.
On Manning Park beach with you, I see you having fun.
I guess something to keep close is to remember the sun.
Many summers together, you made things bright,
Being the captain of lacrosse or smashing Auntie April in
the Marco polo fight.
What about singing together the "burning ring of fire"
with Johnny Cash,
A moment we shared a moment that lasts
You even learned to cook and create new meals,
A trait passed on from Mom and Dad—good deal!
In Cuba, our holiday, we could hear your laugh from
anywhere.
Your mother would say, "Oh there he is. That is Reid
over there."
I saw you grow into this fine young man of these years,
Different experiences, some happy and some with tears.
There is nothing more gratifying then to see your child
move on to build a life,
Like seeing the robins leave the nest and take flight.
You have such a wonderful woman to be by your side:
Abbie, to talk, to share and confide.

It is also amazing she is as tall as you,
A perfect fit for the path of new.
Life together will bring many different things,
Bounded by love represented by these rings.
Embrace this union with all your being,
For this gives such strength and meaning.
A ring is a circle encompassing you both,
Everlasting love, everlasting growth.

Love, Auntie April
Morgyn and Konrad

That Special Friend

Marnie, you are a special friend with a heart of gold,
A precious friend to me to ever hold.
How does one walk into a person's soul,
taking care as she walks along the way
It is you, Marnie, who loves even the smallest
being, giving love to whatever is living
In your presence, you allow me to be me, not
having to change or live up to a theme.
I want to thank you for your eyes in times of stress,
Especially with my son Konrad
when things were a mess.
I will remember this always: To
put on the Marnie glasses
When I need some clarity until the time passes.
My trials with men over these years we have shared;
You have helped me heal the wounds
that hurt and flared.
We laugh so much all the time, which
makes this life absolutely divine.
You catch me when I say "Good"—yet
I haven't got a clue, and it shows.
You caught me in the moment it took place.
I laugh at myself and redeem my grace.
For really that is all most need in life: to laugh
and be human, not that perfect face.
I think what is so really special is that we
share each other's place to grow,
Removing obstacles and truly relishing in the flow.

I know that I have helped you too, and
I see beyond the big girl outside
This is only a reflection of your big heart inside.
Time to own this for yourself, drop
others' pain and enjoy letting go.
It is so nice to finally realize that every
person does their own reap and sow.
You told me of your talent in golf that is natural.
You sacrificed yourself because you
felt bad for the incapable.
What a reflection it is that is in the world of now,
So choose to be that special one and allow.
It is wonderful that we shared each other's eyes,
to see the demolition of our own self-demise,
And here you are in that treasured place of now
To fill that promise, that unspoken vow.
You being the best that you can be is all
that anyone could ask and happily see.
Oh, there will be the ones who try to take you down,
By convincing you to take on their frown.
But now you own your gift for thee, that which
no one can take which has set you free.

The Little Things

How do the little things affect everything?
It could be the little thoughts that live in the mind and sing.
Pay attention to the little things that say, "Stop what you are doing,"
For this is truth of new events ensuing.
My mind sends little things that I wonder are true,
Questioning me in me, who is who.
I fight for the past comforts of being for me,
But I want something different from what I see.
This burning in my soul for true love is daunting to expose.
Maybe this is the lesson: just to open in truth and not to pose.
A life of acting has kept me in the wrong place,
Now my body said, "Stop and take a look at what you have to face."
It has been so hard on my own for twelve years, but I guess I chose this for my soul.
This knowledge comes to me like great wisdom on a treasured scroll.
I saw myself as weak, and wanted to learn
That I deserve approval and have a say,
So I have experienced that in my own way.
Now I am ready for true love of the lessons infused.
Watch the little things that unravel and show,
Releasing tension and going with the flow
All things matter, big or small; it is part of the whole to become tall.

The Man On The Street

You walk by me almost every day.
I wonder to myself, *Is this your path of today?*
I cannot be a judge, but I feel something sad.
It moves deep within me and makes me really mad.
How does this happen in front of my eyes—
Despair I see, or maybe it is lies?
I bet I have seen you for more than ten years,
Walking the same road, in the same clothes, it appears.

I finally said that I have to talk to
you, get through somehow,
See if your gift inside will be lit and allow,
For this gift must be magnificent for
all that you have endured.
You must give it away for others to be cured.

Our hearts are tied in some way I cannot explain—
This compelling urge to acknowledge your pain.

I don't know why I am doing this.
I can't help myself; you cannot be missed.
I recently learned that I cannot understand,
But I can make a difference by taking a stand.
Perhaps these are the words that you need to hear.
My god, I feel it so rich and sincere.
I cannot look the other way; I must do
what I can and say what I say.
I hope you hear me to heal in the deepest way,
Taking you in a new direction, one that will pay.
Let the words drift in like a soft summer rain,
Soaking and soothing, washing away the pain.

Back on the Road, My Son

You were one year old, prancing around, a
delight to anyone who was within sight.
You brought smiles and ease to everyone's life.
Your spirit is delightful, with a
calming knowing of truth,
That which you give with abandon and deep root.
I am blessed to have you as my son,
straight from day one,
Even through the pain to join this world as my son.

When you got sick at a year old, so
precious to take this fall,
I remember after the operation, you
danced and brought smiles to all.
I marveled at this display of magnificence,
This determined display of persistence.

You continue in life, and I say your spirit
comes together, gives you grace.
You take it in with the love that is placed.
You teach me too, my beloved son.
I made mistakes too, although what is done is done.
I remember your words at eleven years
old. "Move on," said my son—
A profound statement for a wise young one.
Then along comes the age of seventeen,
Making life-changing choices being a teen.
Your heart was broken, and you fell
Hard and deep, lost in the well.

This evil of wrong words spoken
Misleads the heart for what was woven.

Your turmoil shook your foundation of belief.
You landed in a pool of rage and reprieve.
So as a mother I come in to save you,
Honestly feeling like this is the right thing to do.
The terror I felt that you could have died
Can't let go this obligation so tied.
When I gave you your space,
You then found the right place.
Your receiving of this knowledge of
self-being so young is gold.
Deeper thinker you are, son, that many do not hold.
You are now a teacher, strong and bold.
Your motto is the truth and will be told.
Your heart now healed attracts that which is earned.
You will be amazed by the lady who stops and turns,
Happiness, naturally, no fight or concern.
Be open, my son, to life's wonderful gifts,
Which will always support you and give you a lift.

Love, Mom

Dad

Dad, I forgive you for the time we have missed.
I forgive you for the wrong things said.
I forgive you for mistakes in the past; they are dead.
I realize the love you have for me,
For my heart is the same with my children, you see.
I accept you now the way that you are,
Your uniqueness is only that of a star.
Dad, I will tell you this now, which seems hard to say:
I love you dearly in my own special way.
You have given me a strength that I can't explain,
And I remember you said to be proud of my name.
Life hands us all great lessons to learn,
Some upfront, some hard to discern.
Dad, I know your Dad didn't show his love when you were a kid.
The pain you endured has been so great, but you have lived,
And that is, at this moment, what counts, and you have a chance to share
All that life taught you, with none to spare.
In understanding at this time what has happened here,
I hope we can be closer than ever this year.
Open your mind and your wisdom to me
So to nourish the tools to be greater than thee.
Maybe through *me* your gifts will go on,
And peace will be yours, and we will all have won.
Love Your Eldest April

I Be
I Am
I Say
I Do

I start each day through the eyes and heart of my inner child,
And all the relationships I desire begin to grow wild.
Encouragement in myself first, and then to others in giving
Is my true reason for living.
Morgyn, my daughter, and my son, Konrad,
Give me purpose I longed for and thought I never had.
I am like a lighthouse in the middle of the night,
Giving guidance and strength, a path I follow in light.
Oh, Mother Nature valued wisdom in what you give to me,
And Father Time is so precious to enjoy being free.
I close my eyes and look through my heart,
A guarantee that this day has a wonderful start.

I should

Should is a message from the past, feeling like I am always last.
I am obligated and feeling under pressure to make things right,
Trying to lift myself up and gain new sight.
I should have known better, and I should have done better.
By the time I say this to myself, it hits like a hammer;
The words continue to go on in a festive yammer,
Circling around, keeping me in an emotional stammer.
I know I should, but it doesn't feel good.
Who is this should?
What is this should?
Why is this should?
How do I do should?
The voice of should commands me to mourn,
Put the dummy cap on and accept the scorn.
So this is who you are, keeping me in pieces and torn—
One of control, repent, and a dark faceless scowl.
I think you must leave and be quiet, don't howl.
You pretend to be big, but you are actually very small.
I admire your strength and the mask of being tall.
The sprinkle of could washes you away.
I am quite excited to find it was so easy in play
To know what I have been, was, said, and done,
Just a myth of battles that can never be won.
Could is the bridge, the one that is stable,
Sturdy, and strong, showing I am able.

Nothing and Everything—Delighted

The great darkness expanded everywhere; there was
nothing—yet something—or is it everything?
No boundaries, free flowing, being, and
reaching—never ending—yet it is one thing.
A thought enters the darkness, and
there was a casting of light,
This beauty revealed gave her meaning,
and in holding this, there was sight.

In this meeting of the great forces
of life—what do we know?
A new insight emerges out of this—
connect in love, which it does bestow.
You, great mother, give depth and understanding,
and you, great father, show the service.
The daughter gives excitement, and they
connect—the ultimate of meaning and purpose

Cries of joy, lightning, rain pours down in huge
droplets, targeting the place of growth.
She opens and receives all that is given in his
mighty strength for the passion of the heart.
Many seeds are tossed around in the
winds of chaos in the storm.
Daughter continues to dance and
celebrate the unity of norm.
The knowing that this is what is all to be, not
a foreign eye of ego to distort the see.

She knows and laughs, because it is all
to be—my "I" and not flee.
Goodbye to ego, unless you support thee to be me.

A calling is put forth, and the great
warrior comes through.
He ventures forward and brings the knowledge intact,
For the seed has flourished in him which shows,
Making footprints for all to follow and grow.

The sun is bright, and he stands
tall in the field of willows.
The bruises on his neck unseen—long gone billows.
A gentle breeze brushes his face
like a soft, warm feather,
And his heart is full of love to stay forever.
For the voice of this brave moved to warrior in fruition,
Fulfilling the long, hard journey
from the light of vision.
One becomes all as they deliver penitence,
Thus follow this warrior with deep reverence.
The stillness takes its place in the knowing
It is what it is the love for bestowing,
The now to become one in unity designed.
The heart leads with no map of a sign;
The ego falls away to open to light
Guided trust, and with this there is no fight.
The beauty unfolds and leads the way,
Letting go of tomorrow and yesterday.
The wonder and devotion needs no words said;
It is the heartbeat that speaks more volumes instead.

Released from the forest of darkness past,
The weight on the warrior falls
easily from his shoulders.
Lightness, new passage is now before him.
The warrior claims his true love of faith.
"All is served. Walk on," says the saint.
For it is to be with thee, for all to see
In glory, united in life, together as one.
Finally, peace, the long awaited outcome.
Surrendering in Love.

A celebration of Willow and Feather, and so it is.

Transformation

How does the transformation begin? Is it something that
occurs from within?
Is it something that is truly living?
Is it something that is truly hidden?
Is it something that is only given?
Am I to receive such a gift?
Do I deserve, or is it a myth?

Nature is being the foundation, the place that is.
I am part of this, and so often in my mind, such a quiz:
What is my Earth like? I have weeds that I continue to extract
To no ending—they keep coming back.
"Okay," I say to myself. "That is just the way it is; that is
who I am."
To which I add, "I am not a fan."
Close my eyes and heart so it will go away, but relentless,
this soul to show me the way.

A dusting of knowledge comes my way. An act of kindness
reaches in,
Creates a crack in the wall, and lets in some light
To loosen my hold, to no longer fight.
I am tired but open to hear from within,
To see my foundation of what has been built in.
I discover and learn that to unlearn is the direction to head,
Instead of looking for the weeds, plant more flowers instead;
Creating and allowing natural growth to do its task,
Instead of plucking and picking, enduring the wrath.
Once the flowers begin to grow, then life begins to flow.

I be, I am, I say, I do are one together balanced to grow.
This is true, my foundation is stronger:
More friends, nice things, and things to ponder.
Creating myself again is a loving act, to evolve and transform.
Dropping old coats of many years worn,
Light yet strong, protected and true, Authentic self—it's
okay to be you.
April

ABOUT THE AUTHOR

In a permanent relationship at nineteen, then married and mother of two, April realized that being miserable is actually a choice, so she chose to change things.

The path to self-awareness took many forms: fire walking, hanging off a cliff, bungee jumping, personal development seminars, and even being a stand-up comic!

In 2005, things started to come together with the discovery of a program or "way of thinking" that would help people realize their full potential and find emotional balance. She has been involved with Toastmasters, speaking about her journey of self-discovery.

April has spent the past ten years developing and refining the program in this book so that you, too, can start on your own path of self-discovery and live a happier and more fulfilling life. April brings the poems in as her own expression, the author's unique way of bringing the mind and the heart together.

RECOMMENDED READING LIST

The Essential Law of Attraction Collection
by Esther and Jerry Hicks

Assertiveness for Earth Angels
by Doreen Virtue

Angels of Abundance
by Doreen Virtue and Grant Virtue

Invisible Acts of Power
by Caroline Myss

Getting Real
by Susan Campbell, Ph.D.

The Five Levels of Attachment
by Don Miguel Ruiz Jr.

Dying to Be Me
by Anita Moorjani

You'll See It When You Believe It
by Wayne Dyer

Living Your Yoga
by Judith Lasater, Ph.D., P.T.

The Gift of Change
by Marianne Williamson

The Seat of the Soul
by Gary Zukav

The Alchemist
by Paulo Coelho

Heal Your Body
by Louise L. Hay

The next book: *I Is, I Have, I Converse, and I Relate.*

The next level of aspect of self: 5,6,7,8, the Pentad, Hexad, Heptad, and Octad.

SUMMARY

The "Tetrad Eyes" is a system for making changes at the four aspects of self: your beingness, identity, expression, and actions. Symbolism brings a deeper understanding. The Monad is totality, oneness, and that is why each aspect is within one circle. The four aspects of self are represented in one circle to be looked at all at the same time. It is not possible to change one aspect of self without affecting the other three. This requires whole-mind awareness. This is illustrated in the Full Integrity Circle. The Full Integrity Circle, encompasses all the symbols: the Monad, Dyad, Triad, and Tetrad. The chapter "Why Symbols" shows in black lettering the Negative mind. A person must bring attention to these thoughts to get out of the Ego, which then results in a unified self.

With the practice of paying consideration to the bad-feeling thoughts at each aspect, these parts of self will be repaired. Each thought has a feeling to it, and when you plot it in the system, you can see the connections of how one thought hurts all four aspects of self. The mind likes to know where it is going.

You take the negative thought and replace it with the exact opposite statement. The feelings change at this point. Instead of being stuck in polarity, the benefits of opposites show up. The purpose of the Triad is to show the resolution. What ever thought that you have that does not feel good can be reformed. You then act differently and have a more gratifying life. Sharing poems along the way is a different perspective of bringing the heart and mind together.

Printed in the United States
By Bookmasters